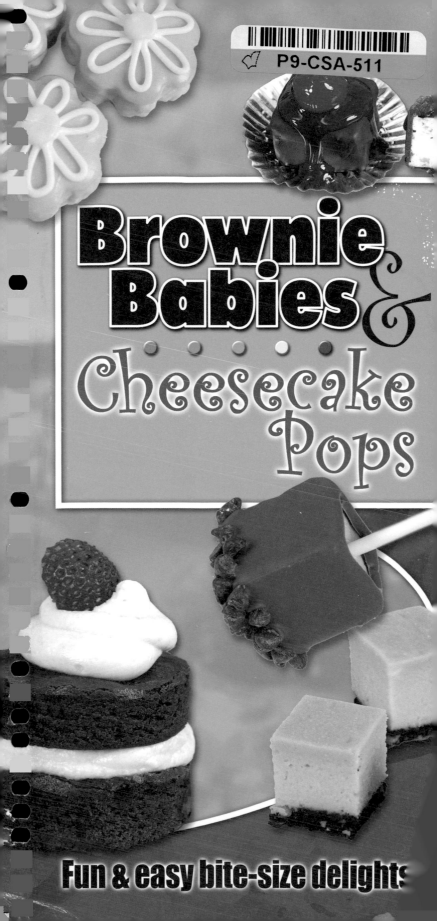

P9-CSA-511

Brownie Babies & Cheesecake Pops

Fun & easy bite-size delights

Printed in the United States of America
by G&R Publishing Co.

Published By:

CQProducts

507 Industrial Street
Waverly, IA 50677

ISBN-13: 978-1-56383-364-9
SBN-10: 1-56383-364-6
em #7048

Table of Contents

Getting Started

Bite-size brownies and cheesecakes are the answer to dessert deprivation! Guests can indulge in more than one tiny treat without any guilt. And preparation is easy because these small desserts generally bake more quickly than the full-size versions. Many can be assembled ahead of time and frozen for later use. Simply thaw them before serving.

To create an impressive assortment of mini desserts for a party, look for "Instant Party Platters" throughout the book. Start with one recipe and give it several twists using the delicious variations that are included. It's "no biggie" to turn plain into party-perfect every time with these fun and easy bite-size delights!

Brownie Tips

- In place of specialty baking pans, brownies may be baked in round, square or rectangular pans and then cut with a knife or cookie cutters into desired shapes before decorating.

- "Testing done" is achieved when a toothpick inserted halfway between the center and edge of pan comes out with few or no crumbs.

- If brownies do not immediately adhere to lollipop sticks when making brownie pops, simply press the brownie gently against the stick or refrigerate pops for 30 minutes until adhered.

- Lining pans with aluminum foil or parchment paper before baking allows easy removal from the pan for trouble-free cutting.

- For easier handling, refrigerate brownie cut-outs on the sticks before dipping, drizzling or coating with melted mixtures.

- Use a plastic knife to cut dense, chewy brownies.

- Use a wire cooling rack to cool brownies quickly.

- Place waxed paper under a cooling rack to catch the drips when drizzling brownies with icing or melted almond bark. If coated brownies are set directly on waxed paper to dry, coating may puddle. Carefully cut away the excess coating after it dries.

Cheesecake Tips

- For the smoothest cheesecakes, begin with cream cheese that has been softened at room temperature. Beat it with an electric mixer just until smooth and creamy before adding any other ingredients.

- Short on time? Unwrap the cream cheese and place it in a microwave-safe bowl to warm on low power just until softened.

- Use eggs at room temperature.

- Baking cheesecakes in a hot water bath may prevent cracking on top. However, most mini cheesecakes will be garnished on top so a small amount of cracking should not affect finished appearance.

- Most mini cheesecakes will settle upon cooling. This can provide space for garnishes.

- Cheesecake pops and miniatures should be served chilled.

Equipment Tips

Mini cheesecake pans:

- Purchase good quality, nonstick pans with removable metal disks in the base of each cup.

- If a cheesecake crust contains butter or margarine, set a jellyroll pan underneath to catch any drips during baking.

- To remove cheesecakes or brownies from pan, loosen outer edges with a toothpick or thin knife as needed and push up on the disk in each cup to slide the dessert out. Remove the disk before serving.

Small springform pans:

- Purchase good quality, nonstick pans with easy-to-manipulate hinges on the outside.

- If pans are not completely tight, securely wrap the bottom in heavy-duty foil if baking the cheesecakes in a hot water bath.

Other supplies:

- Mini muffin pans can be purchased with 12 or 24 cups. Decorative mini cupcake liners (paper and foil) are available in many styles and colors at most kitchen shops, department stores or online stores.

- White *lollipop* sticks are generally about 4″ long and are heat-safe; plastic ones should be inserted after baking. White *cookie* sticks are somewhat thicker. These and other supplies can be found wherever baking and cake decorating supplies are sold. Always purchase items that are food-safe.

- Miniature cookie cutters can be used to cut brownies and cheese-cakes into fun shapes. Metal petit four cutters are approximately 1¼″ in diameter and 2″ tall, making them perfect for tiny desserts.

Instant Party Platter

For an impressive party platter, start with one or two basic recipes in this book, and then use the suggestions and variations following the recipes to create a wide assortment of bite-size desserts. It only looks difficult!

Chocolate-Covered Cheesecake Pops

Makes about 2½ dozen

Filling

2 (8 oz.) pkgs. cream cheese, softened

¾ C. sugar

1½ T. flour

2 eggs

1 egg yolk

½ C. sour cream

1½ tsp. vanilla extract

1½ tsp. lemon juice

Coating **&** Garnishes

⅓ C. white candy melts wafers (or almond bark)

1 (12 oz.) pkg. dark chocolate or semi-sweet chocolate chips

1 T. shortening

Colored candy sprinkles

Ribbons to match

Equipment
9″ round baking pan, small cookie scoop, sheet of Styrofoam, white lollipop sticks

Preheat oven to 325°. Coat pan with nonstick cooking spray. In a medium mixing bowl, beat the cream cheese at medium speed until smooth. Add sugar and flour; beat until light and fluffy. Reduce speed and add eggs; mix well. Mix in sour cream, vanilla extract and lemon juice until combined. Spread mixture in prepared pan. Set the pan in a hot water bath* and bake for approximately 40 minutes. Remove pan from water bath and cool cheesecake to room temperature. Cover and refrigerate for 3 hours or overnight.

When cheesecake is cold and firm, scoop out small balls from the pan. Roll with damp hands to shape smoothly. Heat candy melts (about 25 wafers) in the microwave until melted and smooth. Carefully insert a lollipop stick halfway into each cheesecake ball, pull it out and drizzle a

> * To make a hot water bath, set the baking pan in a larger roasting pan. Fill the roasting pan with boiling water until it reaches about halfway up the sides of the cake pan.

little melted candy into each hole. Re-insert sticks. Freeze cheesecake pops for at least 1 hour.

Melt chocolate chips and shortening in the microwave until smooth. Spoon melted chocolate over each cheesecake pop, covering as much as desired. While chocolate is still wet, scatter candy sprinkles over the top. Push sticks into a sheet of Styrofoam until chocolate sets. Tie curly ribbon around each stick before serving. Pops may be refrigerated for a short time before serving if necessary.

Serving Suggestions

- Cut a piece of Styrofoam to fit into a container, at least 3″ deep. Cover foam with foil. (If using a glass container, leave space between foam and inside edges.) Fill container with colored jellybeans and push ends of lollipop sticks into foam.

- Set cheesecake pops, with sticks up, in mini paper or foil cupcake liners or directly on a serving platter.

- Omit lollipop sticks and set cheesecake balls in decorative mini cupcake liners.

Variations

Itty Bitty Bites

Prepare, bake and chill cheesecake as directed. Using a small round cookie cutter (1¼″ to 2″), cut out small disks of cheesecake. Dip bottoms and/or sides in tiny candy or sugar sprinkles and serve on a platter or in pretty paper liners.

Instant Party Platter

Use half the pan of prepared cheesecake to cut out Itty Bitty Bites, using 1″ to 1½″ round, oval and flower-shaped cookie cutters; decorate the bottoms or sides with sprinkles as desired. Use the remaining cheesecake to make Chocolate Covered Cheesecake Pops. Coat the pops in different colors of melted candy wafers, chocolate or almond bark, and then decorate with colored sprinkles and tie with coordinating ribbons. Arrange the assortment on one platter to serve.

Peppermint Brownie Pops

Makes about 2½ dozen

Brownies

6 oz. bittersweet
    baking chocolate

2 oz. unsweetened
    baking chocolate

¾ C. butter

1½ C. sugar

2½ tsp. vanilla extract

4 eggs

1 C. flour

¼ tsp. salt

1 T. crushed
    peppermint candy

¾ C. semi-sweet
    chocolate chips

Coating&Garnishes

12 squares vanilla-flavored
    almond bark

Additional crushed
    peppermint candy

Equipment brownie pops pan(s), white lollipop sticks
or mini candy canes

Preheat oven to 350°. Lightly coat pans with nonstick cooking spray.
Set pan(s) on a cookie sheet for easy handling.

Melt bittersweet chocolate, unsweetened chocolate and butter in the
microwave until smooth. Add sugar and vanilla extract, mixing until
smooth. Stir in eggs, one at a time, until well mixed. Stir in flour and salt.
Fold in candy and chocolate chips. Fill brownie pop molds about ¾ full.
Bake 25 minutes or until a few crumbs stick to a toothpick inserted into
center of brownie pop. Place pan on cooling rack until nearly cool.
Carefully run a toothpick or butter knife around each brownie pop to
loosen from pan, if needed. Invert pan to remove pops, applying gentle
pressure to the bottom. Turn the brownies, flat side down, on waxed
paper; insert sticks or candy canes from the top to within about ½″ of
the bottom of the pop. Cool completely.

In a small narrow bowl, melt three almond bark squares in the microwave until smooth. Place crushed peppermints in a small bowl. Lift the brownie pops carefully by the stick and dip into the melted bark, coating each pop about halfway. Immediately sprinkle with crushed candy. Set on waxed paper to dry. Working in batches, repeat with remaining brownie pops, almond bark and candy.

Instant Party Platter

To create a variety of flavors, divide the brownie batter evenly between four small bowls. Stir one of the following into each bowl: ¾ teaspoon crushed peppermint candy, ¾ teaspoon instant coffee granules, 1-2 teaspoons toffee bits and 1-2 teaspoons crushed nuts. Bake as directed and dip pops into any pleasing combination of the following: melted chocolate- or vanilla-flavored almond bark followed by crushed peppermint candy, crushed toffee bits, crushed nuts or chocolate sprinkles.

To get a different look, make only 24 brownie pops and save ¼ of the batter to prepare Brownie Stacks as directed on the following page.

Brownie Stacks

Makes about 1 dozen

Brownies

¼ of the batter* from Peppermint Brownie Pops (recipe, page 8)

Frosting

¼ C. shortening	¼ tsp. butter flavoring
Dash salt	Egg white powder and water to equal ½ egg white (following package instructions)
1¼ C. powdered sugar, sifted	
¼ tsp. clear vanilla extract	
½ tsp. almond extract	Red food coloring

Equipment 8 x 8″ baking pan, plastic piping bag with tips

Preheat oven to 350°. Line pan with parchment paper, allowing 2″ to hang over all sides of pan. Spread ¼ of the batter from Peppermint Brownie Pops (recipe page 8) into prepared pan. Bake 20 minutes or until brownies test done. Let cool. Gripping parchment paper, remove cooled brownies from pan. Using a 1″ to 1½″ round cookie cutter, cut as many rounds as possible.

To make frosting, beat shortening at medium speed until creamy. Add 2 teaspoons hot water, salt, powdered sugar, vanilla, almond extract, butter flavoring and egg white ingredients. Beat until well mixed and piping consistency is achieved. Blend in food coloring. Spoon mixture into a plastic piping bag fitted with a large round tip. Pipe frosting on one brownie round and stack another round on top. Create additional stacks of two or three rounds, with frosting between layers.

> * For a larger batch of brownie stacks, use half of the brownie batter from page 8 in a 9 x 13″ baking pan. To use the full brownie recipe, divide batter between two 9 x 13″ pans and double the buttercream frosting recipe.

Milk Chocolate Malt Cheesecakes

Makes 3 to 3½ dozen

Crust

½ C. finely crushed chocolate graham cracker crumbs

2¼ tsp. melted butter

Filling

¼ C. heavy whipping cream

¼ C. malted milk powder

1 C. milk chocolate chips

2 (8 oz.) pkgs. cream cheese, softened

½ C. sugar

2 eggs

½ C. sour cream

1 tsp. vanilla extract

Topping & Garnish

2½ C. sweetened whipped cream or whipped topping

Milk chocolate shavings

Equipment

nonstick mini muffin pan(s), optional plastic piping bag and tips

Preheat oven to 350°. Coat muffin cups with nonstick cooking spray. In a small bowl, combine crumbs and butter. Spoon ½ to 1 teaspoon crumb mixture into each muffin cup; press firmly against bottom. Pour cream into a glass measuring cup and microwave for 40 seconds or until very warm. Stir in malt powder to dissolve. Let mixture stand for 5 to 10 minutes and then strain the cream. Melt chocolate chips in microwave and stir until smooth; set aside. In a medium mixing bowl, beat cream cheese at medium speed until smooth. Add sugar and mix well. Reduce speed and add eggs; beat until blended. Mix in sour cream and vanilla extract. Stir in strained cream. Mix in chocolate. Spoon batter into prepared pan over crusts, filling cups about ¾ full. Bake for 14 to 16 minutes or until set. Cool completely. Cover and refrigerate for 4 to 6 hours. Remove cheesecakes from pan. Pipe or place a dollop of whipped cream or topping on each cheesecake and garnish with shaved milk chocolate.

Surprise Brownie Babies

Makes about 2 dozen

Brownies

3 oz. unsweetened baking chocolate, chopped

⅓ C. butter

1 C. sugar

2 eggs, lightly beaten

1 tsp. vanilla extract

½ C. flour

Surprise Centers

24 Hershey's Hugs candies

Equipment

nonstick mini muffin pan(s), mini cupcake liners

Preheat oven to 350°. Insert liners in pans; set aside. Melt chocolate and butter in the microwave until smooth. Add sugar, eggs and vanilla extract; beat lightly until just combined. Stir in flour. Spoon about 1 tablespoon of batter into each muffin cup. Press one unwrapped candy into the center of each brownie.

Bake for 13 to 17 minutes or until a toothpick inserted between the candy and the edge of the pan comes out with a little batter. The brownies will continue to bake after they are removed from the oven. Let cool and decorate*, if desired.

* Use one of the many frosting options on other pages of this book, sprinkle with powdered sugar or leave undecorated to let the surprise center become the star of the show.

Instant Party Platter

Try different "surprise" centers to create and serve an assortment of brownie babies on one platter:

- mini peanut butter cups
- maraschino cherries
- mini candy bars
- other Hugs or Kisses candy varieties

Tips

- *Hugs and Kisses candies are available in a variety of different flavors. Since they stay intact when baked, try using multi-colored or light-colored ones for visual interest when eaten.*

- *When available, try holiday-themed candy.*

Orange-Kissed Brownie Wedges

Makes 1½ to 3 dozen

Brownies

2 eggs	½ C. unsweetened cocoa powder
1 C. sugar	
⅔ C. flour	½ C. butter, melted

Frosting & Glaze

2 T. butter, softened	Orange food coloring
½ tsp. finely shredded orange peel	2 oz. semi-sweet baking chocolate
1¾ C. powdered sugar, divided	¼ C. butter
1 to 1½ T. orange juice, divided	

Equipment 3 (4″) nonstick springform pans

Preheat oven to 350°. Lightly coat pans with nonstick cooking spray; set aside. In a medium mixing bowl, combine eggs and sugar. Beat at medium speed for 3 to 5 minutes or until thickened. Add flour and cocoa to egg mixture, beating just until smooth. Stir in melted butter until combined. Divide batter evenly between prepared pans. Bake for 25 to 30 minutes or until brownies test done. Cool completely in pans.

In a large mixing bowl, combine softened butter and orange peel. Add ½ cup powdered sugar and ½ tablespoon orange juice; beat on medium speed until blended. Beat in remaining 1¼ cups powdered sugar and enough orange juice to make a spreading consistency. Stir in food coloring. Spread frosting on cooled brownies in pans. Cover and chill 30 minutes.

Melt chocolate and ¼ cup butter in microwave until smooth. Cool 15 minutes. Spread chocolate over brownies. Chill 30 minutes to set glaze.

Remove brownies from pans. Cut into 6 to 8 wedges before serving.

Cranberry Blondies

Makes 3 to 5 dozen

Blondies

¾ C. butter, melted

1½ C. brown sugar

2 eggs

¾ tsp. vanilla extract

2¼ C. flour

1½ tsp. baking powder

¼ tsp. salt

⅛ tsp. ground cinnamon

½ C. dried cranberries

1 C. white baking chips

Frosting&Garnish

1 (8 oz.) pkg. cream cheese, softened

1 C. powdered sugar, sifted

1 T. grated orange peel

6 oz. white baking chocolate, melted

½ C. chopped dried cranberries

Equipment 9 x 13″ nonstick baking pan

Preheat oven to 350°. Coat pan with nonstick cooking spray. In a large bowl, combine butter and brown sugar; cool to room temperature. Beat in eggs and vanilla. In a small bowl, combine flour, baking powder, salt and cinnamon; gradually add to butter mixture. Stir in ½ cup cranberries and white baking chips. Spread batter in prepared pan and bake for 18 to 21 minutes or until blondies test done; cool.

In a medium mixing bowl, beat cream cheese until smooth. Mix in powdered sugar and orange peel. Gradually add half the melted chocolate, beating until blended. Spread frosting over blondies. Cut into small rectangles or squares. Sprinkle with chopped cranberries and drizzle with remaining melted chocolate. Immediately remove from pan. Store in refrigerator.

Variation

Use chopped dried apricots in place of the cranberries to make Apricot Blondies.

Chocolate-Covered Brownie Bites

Makes about 2½ dozen

Brownies

1 (19.8 oz.) pkg. brownie
mix, any variety

Water, eggs and oil as
directed on package

Chocolate Topping

1 (14 oz.) can sweetened
condensed milk

8 oz. semi-sweet baking
chocolate

1 tsp. vanilla extract

1 tsp. butter

Equipment 9 x 13˝ nonstick baking pan

Preheat oven to 350°. Lightly coat pan with nonstick cooking spray.
Combine brownie mix, water, eggs and oil as directed on package for
fudgy brownies. Bake according to directions. Remove from oven and let
cool slightly, until easy to handle but still warm. Cut brownies into about
30 squares. (You may wish to cut away the outer edges of the brownies
first as these harder pieces do not roll into balls easily.) Remove from
pan and roll each square into a ball; cool.

In a small saucepan, slowly heat sweetened condensed milk and baking
chocolate until chocolate is melted and mixture is smooth. Add vanilla
and butter; mix well. Place brownie balls on a cooling rack over waxed
paper. Keeping the chocolate warm over hot water, carefully spoon some chocolate over each ball, letting
it drizzle over the edges. Reserve remaining
topping for another use (such as Cherry
Swirls on page 32). Decorate as desired
with ready-to-use icings.

Tip

*This chocolate topping does not set up solidly so move brownie
bites carefully using two forks or a spatula.*

Chocolate & Mint Cheesecake Bites

Makes about 1½ dozen

Crust

1 C. finely crushed chocolate wafer crumbs

2 T. margarine, melted

2 T. sugar

Filling

2 (8 oz.) pkgs. cream cheese, softened

¾ C. sugar

2 eggs

½ tsp. vanilla or mint extract

⅓ C. mint (green) baking chips, melted

Green food coloring

⅓ C. dark chocolate and mint chips, chopped

Topping & Garnish

Chocolate Topping (recipe on page 16) or 1 C. chocolate chips melted with 1 tsp. shortening

Andes mints, broken

Equipment

nonstick mini cheesecake pan(s)

In a small bowl, stir together crumbs, margarine and sugar. Divide mixture between cheesecake cups, using about 2 teaspoons per cup*. Pat crumbs into bottom of cups.

In a medium mixing bowl, beat cream cheese until smooth. Beat in sugar. Reduce speed and add eggs, mixing well. Stir in extract. Divide batter between two bowls. Stir melted mint chips and green food coloring into one bowl. Spoon green mixture into 8 cups in prepared pan, filling almost to the top. Stir chopped chocolate/mint chips into remaining batter. Spoon white mixture into remaining cups. Bake for 17 minutes or until set. Remove from oven and cool completely. Remove cheesecakes from pan(s). Before serving, spoon chocolate topping on each cheesecake and garnish with mint pieces.

> *If using just one mini cheesecake pan, reserve enough crumb mixture for a second batch of 4 to 6 cheesecakes. Chocolate wafer wedges can also be used as a garnish.*

Peanut Butter Cheesecake Pops

Makes 2 to 3 dozen

Crust

1 C. finely crushed chocolate wafer cookie crumbs

⅓ C. peanuts, finely chopped

2 T. margarine, melted

Filling

2 (8 oz.) pkgs. cream cheese, softened

½ C. peanut butter

⅔ C. sugar

4 tsp. flour

½ tsp. vanilla extract

1 egg

1 egg yolk

2 T. heavy cream or half & half

Coating & Garnishes

20 to 24 oz. chocolate-flavored almond bark*

Chopped peanuts, crushed mini M&M baking bits, mini chocolate chips or crushed cookies

Equipment 8 x 8″ baking pan, white lollipop sticks

Preheat oven to 375°. Line pan with foil, pressing bottom and sides as flat and smooth as possible. Coat foil with nonstick cooking spray. In a medium bowl, stir together cookie crumbs, peanuts and margarine. Press mixture into the bottom of prepared baking pan; set aside.

In a large mixing bowl, beat cream cheese at medium speed until smooth, about 30 seconds. Beat in peanut butter. Add sugar, flour and vanilla extract and beat until smooth. Reduce speed, add egg and egg yolk, and beat until well blended. Stir in cream. Pour filling mixture over crust in prepared pan. Place the pan in a larger pan and pour boiling

* For a darker chocolate coating, dip cubes in a mixture of 1 cup chocolate chips (semi-sweet or dark chocolate) melted with 1 to 2 teaspoons shortening.

water into the large pan until it comes halfway up the sides of the 8″ pan. Bake for 40 minutes, then turn off oven and leave cheesecake there for 5 more minutes. Remove cheesecake from water and place on cooling rack. When completely cool, refrigerate for at least 4 hours or overnight.

To make pops, remove cheesecake from pan by lifting up on foil. Peel off foil. Cut cheesecake into small cubes with a long sharp knife, about 1″ on all sides. Push a lollipop stick into the top of each cube and return to the refrigerator or freezer to chill well.

Meanwhile, in a narrow microwave-safe mug, melt 6 ounces of chocolate almond bark* and stir until smooth (for one batch). Arrange chopped nuts, candies or crumbs on small plates for dipping. Holding a cheesecake cube by the stick, dip the end into melted bark, pressing it down until the bark just coats the upper edges. Remove and let excess bark drip off. Dip bottom into desired garnishes and set on waxed paper to dry. Coat six more cubes, spooning bark over top edges as necessary. Repeat with additional batches of almond bark, melting 6 ounces (3 cubes) of bark for each batch of pops.

Instant Party Platter

To serve an assortment of peanut butter cheesecakes on one platter, omit sticks on some cubes and leave them uncoated. Put sticks into remaining cubes and dip them in a variety of chocolate coatings and garnishes. If desired, stir miniature chocolate chips or chopped Reese's Peanut Butter Cups into the batter before baking.

Raspberry Swirl Cheesecake Cubes

Makes about 2 dozen

Crust

½ C. butter, softened
⅔ C. powdered sugar

¼ tsp. salt
1 C. flour

Filling

1 (4 oz.) bar white baking chocolate

1 C. fresh or frozen raspberries

2 (8 oz.) pkgs. cream cheese, softened

½ C. sugar

2 eggs
½ C. sour cream
1 tsp. vanilla extract
Red food coloring
¼ tsp. raspberry extract

Garnishes

½ C. white baking or dark chocolate chips

½ tsp. vegetable oil

Whipped topping and berries, optional

Equipment

8 x 8″ baking pan, plastic bag for piping

Preheat oven to 325°. Line pan with foil, allowing foil to extend about 2″ over pan on all edges. In a medium mixing bowl, beat butter at medium-high speed until creamy. Add powdered sugar and salt; beat 1 minute until light and fluffy. Reduce speed and gradually beat in flour. Press mixture over bottom of prepared pan. Bake for about 18 minutes or until golden brown. Let crust cool on a wire rack.

To make filling, melt white baking chocolate in the microwave until smooth. Set aside to cool to room temperature. Meanwhile, combine raspberries and 1 tablespoon water in a microwave-safe bowl and micro-wave for 1 minute. Press through a strainer set over a bowl to get ¼ cup puree; discard seeds. In a large mixing bowl, beat together cream cheese and sugar at medium-high speed for 2 minutes. Reduce speed and beat in eggs until blended. Beat in sour cream and vanilla.

To raspberry puree, add 1 cup batter, food coloring and raspberry extract; mix well. Remove and reserve ½ cup of mixture. Whisk melted baking chocolate into remaining batter. Pour 1½ cups white batter over cooled crust. Top with spoonfuls of remaining raspberry mixture, then remaining white batter to cover. Top with dollops of reserved raspberry mixture. Drag a toothpick through layers to marbleize. Bake for about 1 hour, until slightly puffed and set. Cool completely, then refrigerate for 1 hour or overnight, until firm.

To serve, lift foil and cheesecake from pan and peel off foil. With a long sharp knife, cut cheesecake into 1⅛″ cubes. Melt white or chocolate chips with oil in the microwave until smooth. Spoon mixture into a plastic bag and cut a tiny piece off one corner for piping. Drizzle lines of chocolate back and forth over the top of each cube. Set cheesecake cubes in miniature paper or foil cupcake liners. Garnish pieces with a dollop of whipped topping and a fresh blueberry or raspberry, if desired. Frilled toothpicks can be used for serving.

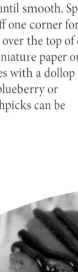

Double-Dipped Blondie Pops

Makes about 2 dozen

Blondies

6 oz. white baking chocolate, broken into pieces

1½ cups flour

½ tsp. baking powder

¼ tsp. salt

¾ C. sugar

2 eggs

⅛ tsp. almond extract

⅓ C. butter, melted and cooled

Coatings & Garnishes

6 oz. vanilla-flavored almond bark

6 oz. chocolate-flavored almond bark

6 oz. caramel bits or caramels

Crushed peanuts

Crushed toffee bits

Decorator sprinkles or nonpareils

Equipment
9 x 9″ nonstick baking pan, white lollipop sticks

Melt white baking chocolate in the microwave until smooth; cool to room temperature. Preheat oven to 350°. Lightly coat pan with nonstick cooking spray. In a small bowl, combine flour, baking powder and salt. In a large bowl, combine sugar, eggs, 2 tablespoons water and almond extract. To the large bowl, add melted chocolate and butter; stir until smooth. Gradually stir in flour mixture and pour into prepared pan. Bake for 24 to 30 minutes or until blondies test done. Let pan cool slightly until easy to handle but still warm.

Cut blondies into about 25 squares. (You may wish to cut away the outer edges of the blondies first as these hard pieces do not roll into balls easily.) Remove from pan and roll each square into a ball. Add a lollipop stick to each and refrigerate.

Place peanuts, toffee bits and sprinkles in three separate small bowls. In separate microwave-safe bowls, place vanilla bark, chocolate bark and caramel bits, adding water to the caramel as directed on package to make a very thin caramel sauce. Working with one flavor of coating at a time, melt it in the microwave until smooth. Dip pops into a melted coating and immediately dip bottom of each pop into one of the garnishes. Reheat coating as needed to maintain a workable consistency. Allow coated pops to dry upright on waxed paper.

Instant Party Platter

Make an assortment of blondie pops by applying a variety of coatings and garnishes in different ways.
- Dip some pops in a single coating and cover completely with finely crushed garnishes.
- Add food coloring to vanilla bark to make a variety of colors.
- Coat some pops in two or three different colors or flavors of coatings. Be sure to let the first coat dry before dipping again. Overlap layers as shown in photo.

Baby Butterfinger Cheesecakes

Makes about 2 dozen

Crust

1 C. finely crushed
vanilla wafers

2 T. sugar

2 T. butter, melted

⅛ tsp. salt

Filling

1 (8 oz.) pkg. cream
cheese, softened

¼ C. creamy
peanut butter

½ C. sugar

1 egg

2 T. heavy cream

⅛ tsp. salt

4 fun size Butterfinger
candy bars, crushed

Topping

1 C. semi-sweet
chocolate chips

2 to 3 T. heavy cream

2 fun size Butterfinger
candy bars, crushed

Equipment

nonstick mini muffin pan(s)
or mini cheesecake pan(s)

Preheat oven to 350°. In a small bowl, combine wafer crumbs, sugar, butter and salt; mix well. Spoon 1 to 3 teaspoons of crumb mixture into each muffin cup or cheesecake cup, pressing it on the bottom and up the sides, if desired. Bake crusts for 8 minutes.

Meanwhile, in a medium mixing bowl, beat cream cheese at medium speed until smooth. Beat in peanut butter. Reduce speed and add sugar, egg, cream and salt; beat until well mixed. Gently fold in crushed candy bars. Spoon some of the mixture into each baked crust, filling muffin cups to the top (approximately 1 teaspoon) or filling cheesecake cups halfway (approximately 1 tablespoon). Bake for 21 to 23 minutes for muffin pans or 25 to 27 minutes for cheesecake pans, or until set. Cool completely before removing from pans.

In a microwave-safe bowl, melt chocolate chips. Stir in enough cream to make mixture smooth and glossy. If needed, microwave mixture for 15 seconds. Spoon chocolate over the top of each cheesecake and sprinkle with crushed candy bar.

Variations

Baby Chocolate Chip Cheesecakes

Replace the vanilla wafers with chocolate chip cookie crumbs. Bake crusts for 8 minutes as before.

Prepare filling as directed but omit crushed Butterfingers, and stir in ½ cup miniature chocolate chips instead. Bake filling for 21 to 23 minutes for muffin pans or 25 to 27 minutes for cheesecake pans, as before.

Use the same chocolate topping.

Baby Scotcheroo Cheesecakes

Replace the vanilla wafers with oatmeal cookie crumbs. Shorten baking time for crust to 6 minutes.

Prepare filling as directed but substitute ¼ cup Nutella spread for the peanut butter. Omit crushed Butterfingers and stir in ¼ cup butterscotch chips and ¼ cup finely chopped peanuts instead. Shorten baking time for filling to 18 minutes.

Use the same chocolate topping.

Instant Party Platter

Prepare one full batch of filling with peanut butter and divide it between two bowls. Stir two crushed Butterfinger candy bars into one bowl. Stir ¼ cup chocolate chip cookie crumbs into remaining bowl. Assemble, bake and garnish before serving.

Dainty Mocha Cheesecake Baskets

Makes about 2 dozen

Crust

½ C. finely crushed
graham cracker crumbs

1 tsp. cocoa powder

24 square wonton wrappers

Filling

1 C. semi-sweet
chocolate chips

1 C. heavy cream

1 (8 oz.) pkg. cream
cheese, softened

2½ T. butter, softened

2½ T. coffee flavored liqueur
(such as Kahlua)*

1 tsp. vanilla extract

Garnishes

Fresh raspberries
or strawberries

Chocolate curls or
chocolate-covered
coffee beans

Equipment   nonstick mini muffin or mini cheesecake pan(s)

Preheat oven to 400°. Coat 24 muffin cups with nonstick cooking spray. In a small bowl, stir together crumbs and cocoa powder. Place wonton wrappers on waxed paper; spray both sides with cooking spray. Sprinkle both sides with crumbs. Place a wrapper in each cup and press down gently until it molds into the cup and tips fan out. (Fill any empty cups in the pan with water to prevent warping.) Bake for 6 to 7 minutes or until golden brown. Cool 15 minutes before removing wonton baskets.

Melt chocolate chips in microwave until smooth. In a small chilled mixing bowl, beat cream at high speed until soft peaks form; set aside. In a medium mixing bowl, beat together cream cheese and butter. Add liqueur, vanilla and chocolate, mixing well. Fold in whipped cream until blended. Spoon filling into wonton baskets and chill for 30 minutes. Garnish as desired before serving.

*For a non-alcoholic substitute, dissolve ½ to 1 teaspoon
instant coffee in 2 tablespoons water.*

No-Bake Mandarin Orange Tartlets

Makes about 2 dozen

Filling

1 (8 oz.) pkg. cream cheese, softened

½ C. sugar

2 T. frozen orange juice concentrate, thawed

1 tsp. orange extract

½ (8 oz.) container extra-creamy whipped topping, thawed

1 tsp. grated orange peel

Crust & Garnish

24 baked mini Phyllo shells

Additional grated orange peel

In a medium mixing bowl, beat cream cheese at medium speed until smooth. Add sugar and beat until light and fluffy. Beat in orange concentrate and orange extract. Fold in whipped topping and 1 teaspoon orange peel until well blended. Spoon a small amount of orange filling into each Phyllo shell and garnish with a sprinkling of additional orange peel. Cover and chill for 30 minutes.

Instant Party Platter

Mix and match the fillings and shells, using additional flavors of your favorite no-bake cheesecakes to make an assortment of tartlets and baskets. Change up the flavor of the wonton baskets by replacing the cocoa powder in the crust mixture with ground cinnamon, or use plain crumbs (recipe on page 26). Garnish each tartlet or basket with small pieces of fruit.

Cream-Filled Fudgies

Makes about 2 dozen

Brownies

1 (18 oz.) pkg. Ghirardelli Ultimate Fudge Brownie Mix

Water, eggs and oil as directed on package

Filling&Frosting

Fluffy Buttercream Frosting (recipe on page 10)

Garnish

Candy sprinkles, optional

Equipment

nonstick mini muffin pan(s), mini cupcake liners, plastic piping bag fitted with a long round tip (Bismarck tip)

Preheat oven to 325°. Combine brownie mix, water, eggs and oil as directed on package. Set liners in pans and fill each cup about ⅔ full. Bake for about 13 minutes or until they test done. Using the fudge packet from the mix (warm the packet as instructed on package), fill half the brownies from the top using a piping bag with a long tip. Pipe or frost tops of brownies with more of the fudge topping. Prepare Fluffy Buttercream Frosting following the recipe on page 10, leaving it white. Put frosting into a piping bag fitted with a long tip, insert tip into the top of each remaining brownie and pipe filling inside. Pipe additional white frosting on top of brownies. Decorate as desired with sprinkles.

Tip

Before serving, set brownies into a second paper liner for a fresh appearance.

Fudgies à la mode

Prepare brownie batter as directed on page 28. Spoon batter into approximately 24 greased mini muffin pan cups, filling about ⅔ full. Bake for 14 to 17 minutes or until they test done. Cool completely. Meanwhile, using a small cookie scoop, scoop 24 balls of ice cream (various flavors) onto a waxed-paper lined tray. Freeze at least one hour or until ready to serve. Just before serving, remove brownies from pan(s) and set each one in a party nut cup. Top with ice cream, garnish as desired and serve immediately.

Instant Party Platter

Bake all the brownies without paper liners. Fill or frost ⅓ of them with buttercream frosting. Fill or frost ⅓ of them with chocolate fudge. Top the remaining brownies with ice cream and set all brownies into an assortment of liners or party nut cups.

Coconut Cheesecake Bon Bons

Makes about 2 dozen

Filling

1½ (8 oz.) pkgs. cream
    cheese, softened
¼ C. sugar
¼ tsp. vanilla extract
⅛ tsp. almond extract

1 egg
1 egg yolk
½ C. sweetened flaked coconut
¼ C. finely ground pecans

Coating & Garnishes

1 C. milk chocolate chips
1 T. shortening

Toasted coconut*
Chopped or ground pecans

Equipment 9″ round nonstick baking pan, mini cupcake
liners, optional small cookie scoop

Preheat oven to 350°. Coat pan with nonstick cooking spray; set aside.
In a medium mixing bowl, beat cream cheese at medium speed until
smooth. Add sugar, vanilla and almond extract, beating until fluffy.
Reduce speed and add egg and egg yolk; beat until combined. Fold
in coconut and pecans. Spread mixture in prepared pan and bake for
30 minutes or until set and just beginning to brown. Cool for
30 minutes, then cover and chill for 4 hours or longer.

To make pops, scoop chilled cheesecake out of pan with a spoon or
small cookie scoop and use hands to roll into balls, about 1¼″ in
diameter. Chill at least 30 minutes in the freezer. Melt chocolate chips
and shortening in the microwave until smooth. Holding a cheesecake
ball on a fork over the bowl, spoon chocolate over ball to coat; tap fork
against bowl to let excess chocolate drip off. Set on waxed paper and
sprinkle with toasted coconut or nuts while wet. Let dry completely.
Serve bon bons in mini cupcake liners.

* To toast, place coconut in a single layer on a baking sheet.
Bake at 350° for 5 to 8 minutes or until golden brown.

Chocolate-Covered Cherry Cheesecake Bits

Makes about 3 dozen

Filling

2 (8 oz.) pkgs. cream
  cheese, softened

⅓ C. sugar

⅓ C. sour cream

1 tsp. vanilla extract

2 eggs

¼ C. finely crushed
  gingersnap cookie crumbs

1 (22 oz.) can cherry pie
  filling, divided

Coating

1½ C. bittersweet, semi-sweet
  or milk chocolate chips

2 T. shortening

Equipment

8 x 8″ baking pan, mini paper or foil cupcake
liners, optional

Preheat oven to 350°. Line pan with foil and coat with nonstick cooking spray. In a medium mixing bowl, beat cream cheese at medium speed until smooth. Beat in sugar gradually. Add sour cream and vanilla; beat until blended. Reduce speed and add eggs, beating until smooth. Fold in crumbs and spread mixture in prepared pan. Bake 40 minutes or until set and lightly browned. Cool for 40 minutes and then refrigerate for at least 2 hours.

Lift foil and cheesecake from pan. Cut off edges to level the top. Lightly score cheesecake into small squares. Press the end of a wooden spoon into the middle of each square, about ¼″ deep. Mash the cherries from half of the pie filling and spread over cheesecake. Freeze for 1 hour.

Cut cheesecake as scored and remove from pan. Melt chocolate chips and shortening in the microwave until smooth. Holding a cheesecake square on a fork over the bowl, spoon chocolate over square until coated; tap fork to let excess chocolate drip off. Set on waxed paper to dry. If desired, garnish with remaining pie filling before serving in paper or foil liners.

Cherry Swirls

Makes 2 to 3 dozen

Brownies

4 oz. unsweetened baking chocolate

1 C. butter

2 C. sugar

2 tsp. vanilla extract

4 eggs

1½ C. flour

½ tsp. salt

Filling

2 (8 oz.) pkgs. cream cheese, softened

½ C. sugar

1 egg

½ C. chopped red maraschino cherries

2 tsp. red maraschino cherry juice

Frosting

1 (16 oz.) container chocolate frosting

Equipment

9 x 13″ nonstick baking pan

Preheat oven to 350°. Lightly coat pan with nonstick cooking spray. Melt chocolate and butter in microwave until smooth; cool 5 minutes. Pour into a large bowl and add 2 cups sugar, vanilla and 4 eggs; beat on medium speed for about 1 minute, scraping bowl occasionally. Blend in flour and salt on low speed until combined, about 30 seconds. Beat on medium speed an additional minute. Pour half of the brownie batter into prepared pan.

In a medium bowl, beat cream cheese until smooth. Add ½ cup sugar, 1 egg, cherries and cherry juice, mixing until smooth. Pour the mixture evenly over the brownie batter. Cover with remaining brownie batter in bowl. With a knife, gently swirl through batters for a marbled design.

Bake for 35 to 40 minutes or until brownies test done. Cool completely. Spread with chocolate frosting (or icing on page 33) and cut into small cubes.

Chocolate Chip Icing

¼ C. sugar

¼ C. brown sugar

2 T. butter

2 T. milk

¼ C. semi-sweet
chocolate chips

In a small saucepan over medium heat, combine sugar, brown sugar, butter and milk. Bring mixture to a rolling boil and cook for 1 minute, stirring constantly. Remove from heat and stir in chocolate chips. Beat icing with a wire whisk until chips are melted and icing is smooth. Immediately spread icing on brownies as this icing sets up very quickly.

Instant Party Platter

To make a holiday pair, lightly coat two 8 x 8" baking pans with nonstick cooking spray. Make brownie batter as directed and spread ¼ in each pan. Prepare filling as directed (without cherries and juice) and divide evenly between two small bowls. To one bowl, add ¼ cup red maraschino cherries and 1 teaspoon red maraschino juice. To the other bowl, add ¼ cup green maraschino cherries and 1 teaspoon green maraschino juice. Stir until smooth. Pour red mixture evenly over one pan of brownie batter and the green mixture evenly over the remaining pan of batter. Cover cherry mixture in both pans with the remaining brownie batter in bowl. Swirl and bake as directed. Prepare or use Chocolate Topping from page 16 to frost one pan of Cherry Swirls. Use Chocolate Chip Icing recipe above to frost remaining pan.

Triple Chocolate Cheesecake Wedges

Makes 2½ to 3 dozen

Crust

2 C. crushed cream-filled
  chocolate sandwich
  cookies (such as Oreos)

2 T. butter, melted

Filling

2 (8 oz.) pkgs. cream
  cheese, softened

½ C. sugar

1 T. flour

½ tsp. vanilla extract

4 (1 oz.) squares semi-sweet
  baking chocolate, melted
  and cooled

2 eggs

Coating

Chocolate-flavored
  almond bark (6 oz. will
  coat 8 wedges)

Vanilla-flavored almond bark
  (6 oz. will coat 8 wedges)

Sparkle gel (red, green)

2 oz. vanilla-flavored almond
  bark (for drizzling)

Equipment

4 (4″) nonstick springform pans,
white lollipop sticks

Preheat oven to 325°. In a medium bowl, stir together cookie crumbs
and melted butter. Lightly coat pans with nonstick cooking spray. Press
½ cup of crumb mixture into the bottom of each springform pan;
set aside. In a medium mixing bowl, beat cream cheese at medium
speed just until smooth. Add sugar, flour and vanilla; beat until well
combined. Mix in melted chocolate. Reduce speed and add eggs, mixing
until blended. Pour ¼ of filling over each crust, smoothing tops. Set
springform pans on a baking sheet with edges. Bake for 38 to 41 minutes
or until set. Cool completely, then refrigerate for 4 hours or overnight.

Remove cheesecake from pan. Cut each cheesecake into eight wedges. Push a lollipop stick into the end of each wedge and refrigerate for at least 30 minutes.

Melt 6 ounces of almond bark in the microwave following package instructions; stir until smooth. Holding a cheesecake wedge on a fork over the bowl, spoon melted bark over the top and sides; tap fork lightly against bowl to let excess bark drip off. Place on waxed paper to dry. Repeat with remaining bark and wedges.

Variations

Peppermint Cheesecake

Crush a candy cane and sprinkle over one crust before adding filling. After baking, chilling and slicing, coat wedges in chocolate almond bark and sprinkle additional crushed candy on top while bark is wet.

Raspberry Cheesecake

Spread 1 tablespoon raspberry preserves over center of one crust before adding filling. After baking, chilling and slicing, coat wedges in vanilla almond bark and drizzle sparkle gel over top as desired.

Instant Party Platter

Prepare crust and filling as directed. Make two plain chocolate pans, one peppermint and one raspberry. Garnish wedges from each pan differently, coating some in chocolate, some in vanilla and leaving others uncoated. Drizzle with contrasting bark or gels and arrange wedges on a round platter with points meeting in the middle.

Brownie Bomb Pops

Makes about 2½ dozen

Brownies

1 (1 oz.) square unsweetened chocolate

1 (3 oz.) pkg. cream cheese, softened

¼ C. butter, softened

¾ C. sugar

2 eggs

⅔ C. flour

½ tsp. baking powder

¼ tsp. salt

Powdered Sugar Icing

2 C. sifted powdered sugar

1 to 2 T. milk

¼ tsp. vanilla extract

Food coloring of choice, optional

Garnish

Nonpareils

Equipment

9 x 9″ baking pan, parchment paper, white cookie sticks, colored drinking straws

Preheat oven to 350°. Line pan with parchment paper, allowing 2″ to hang over all sides of pan. Melt unsweetened chocolate in the microwave until smooth; cool. In a medium mixing bowl, beat cream cheese at medium speed until smooth. Add butter and sugar; mix until smooth. Beat in eggs. In a small bowl, combine flour, baking powder and salt; stir into creamed mixture. Add cooled chocolate; stir to combine. Pour into prepared pan. Bake for 15 to 20 minutes; cool in pan.

Gripping parchment paper, remove cooled brownies from pan. Cut into bars about 1″ wide and 2″ long. Insert a cookie stick into one end of each brownie as far as possible without pushing stick through to the other side.

Mix powdered sugar, milk, vanilla and food coloring, if desired, until smooth and of drizzling consistency. Drizzle icing over three sides of the bomb pops and the end opposite the stick, leaving about ½″ unfrosted near the stick. Sprinkle with nonpareils. Set on a cooling rack or waxed paper until dry. Drizzle icing over the uncoated side to within ½″ of stick, sprinkle with nonpareils and let dry. Slide drinking straw over stick and trim to same length.

Variations

Checkerboard Brownie Bomb Pops

Prepare batter as directed, setting aside the melted and cooled chocolate. Drop half the plain batter from a tablespoon, checkerboard fashion, into prepared pan. To remaining batter in bowl, stir in chocolate. Drop chocolate batter from tablespoon into open spaces in pan. Bake and decorate as directed.

Checkerboard Mint Brownie Bomb Pops

Prepare batter as directed, setting aside the melted and cooled chocolate. Divide batter between two bowls. To one bowl, stir in chocolate. To remaining bowl, add ½ teaspoon peppermint extract and several drops of green food coloring; stir well. Drop half the chocolate batter from a tablespoon, checkerboard fashion, into prepared pan. Drop peppermint batter from tablespoon into open spaces in pan. Bake and decorate as directed.

No-Bake Pumpkin Wedges

Makes about 2 dozen

Crust

1½ C. finely crushed ginger-snap cookie crumbs

3 T. butter, melted

Filling

1 (1 lb. 8.3 oz.) tub refrigerated cheesecake filling

½ (15 oz.) can pumpkin puree

¾ tsp. pumpkin pie spice

Garnishes

Whipped topping

Ground cinnamon or gingersnap crumbs

Toasted pecan halves, optional

Equipment 4 (4″) nonstick springform pans

Lightly coat pans with nonstick cooking spray. In a small bowl, stir together crumbs and butter. Divide mixture evenly among four (4″) springform pans and press firmly into bottom of pans. Bake crust for 7 minutes; cool completely.

Stir cheesecake filling until smooth. Transfer half of the filling to a medium bowl; set aside. Divide and spread remaining filling evenly over the crusts in the springform pans. To filling in the bowl, add pumpkin puree and spice; mix well. Divide and spread pumpkin filling evenly over the plain cheesecake in each pan. Cover and refrigerate at least 4 hours or until set.

To serve, remove pan sides. Cut each cheesecake into six or eight wedges and transfer to a serving platter. Garnish wedges with a dollop of whipped topping and a sprinkling of cinnamon or gingersnap crumbs; add a toasted pecan, if desired.

Strawberry Cheesecake Minis

Makes 1½ to 2 dozen

Crust

1¼ C. finely crushed vanilla
wafer crumbs

2 T. sugar
1½ T. butter, melted

Filling

2 (8 oz.) pkgs. cream
cheese, softened

½ C. sugar

½ tsp. vanilla extract

½ tsp. strawberry flavoring

2 eggs

¼ C. strawberry preserves

Red food coloring

Garnishes

Whipped topping (plain or
strawberry-flavored)

Chocolate filigrees (Refer to
instructions on page 60.)

Equipment

nonstick mini cheesecake
pan(s), plastic bags

Preheat oven to 350°. In a small bowl, stir together crumbs, sugar and melted butter. Firmly press approximately 1 tablespoon of crumb mixture into the bottom of each cheesecake cup; set aside. In a medium mixing bowl, beat cream cheese at medium speed until smooth. Beat in sugar, vanilla and strawberry flavoring. Reduce speed and add eggs, mixing until well blended. Stir in preserves and food coloring to reach desired color. Spoon cheesecake mixture into prepared pan, filling each cup about ⅔ full. Bake for 15 to 18 minutes or until set. Cool completely. Refrigerate 3 hours or overnight. Remove cheesecakes from pan and garnish with a dollop of whipped topping and a chocolate filigree.

Variation

Make Raspberry Cheesecake Minis by using seedless raspberry preserves and flavoring in place of strawberry preserves and flavoring. Garnish with fresh raspberries.

Cookie Crust Cheesecakes

Cherry-Topped Cheesecakes

Makes about 4 dozen

Crust

Small vanilla wafers (or cookies of choice as listed on page 41)

Filling

2 (8 oz.) pkgs. cream cheese, softened	1 tsp. vanilla extract
½ C. sugar	2 eggs

Topping

Cherry pie filling

Equipment

nonstick mini muffin pan(s), mini paper or foil cupcake liners

Preheat oven to 325°. Place liner in each muffin cup and set a wafer in the bottom of each liner. In a medium mixing bowl, beat cream cheese at medium speed until smooth. Beat in sugar and vanilla. Reduce speed and add eggs, beating until blended. Spoon approximately 1 tablespoon of filling over each wafer, filling liners about ¾ full. Bake for 15 to 18 minutes or until set. Let cool completely. Chill for at least 1 hour. Just before serving, top each cheesecake with a small amount of pie filling.

Instant Party Platter

After making the basic cheesecake filling, divide mixture between six bowls (or the number of flavor combinations you wish to make). Stir in a small amount of any of the ingredients on the following page in any combinations you like. Garnish as desired to serve a whole platter of mini cheesecakes in a variety of flavors using one basic recipe.

Variations

Chocolate Chip Cheesecakes

Use small chocolate chip cookies in liners.

Add ¾ cup miniature chocolate chips to filling mixture, fill cups and bake as directed. Drizzle with fudge sauce.

Oreo Cheesecakes

Prop small Oreo cookies on edge in liners.

Add ¾ cup crushed Oreo cookies to filling mixture, fill cups and bake as directed. Garnish with whipped topping and crushed cookies.

Peanut Butter Cheesecakes

Use small Nutter Butter cookies in liners.

Add ½ cup creamy peanut butter to filling mixture, fill cups and bake as directed. Garnish with fudge sauce or cookie crumbles.

Chocolate Cheesecakes

Use Oreo Thin Crisps in liners.

Add ¼ cup unsweetened cocoa powder to filling mixture, fill cups and bake as directed. Garnish with fudge sauce and cookie sprinkles.

Spice Cheesecakes

Use small gingersnaps in liners.

Add 2 teaspoons pumpkin pie spice or ground cinnamon to filling mixture, fill cups and bake as directed. Garnish with whipped topping and finely crushed gingersnaps or ground cinnamon.

Raspberry Moussed Brownies

Makes about 2½ dozen

Brownies

3½ oz. unsweetened baking chocolate, chopped

⅔ C. butter, cut into pieces

1 C. sugar

1 tsp. vanilla extract

¼ tsp. raspberry or almond extract (optional)

2 eggs

½ C. flour

¼ C. unsweetened cocoa powder

½ tsp. baking powder

½ tsp. salt

Mousse Topping

1 env. unflavored gelatin

2 C. heavy cream

⅔ C. sugar

½ C. chopped frozen raspberries, thawed

1 T. raspberry juice

Equipment
nonstick mini muffin pan(s), plastic piping bag with tips, optional

Preheat oven to 350°. Lightly coat muffin pans with nonstick cooking spray. Melt chocolate and butter in microwave until smooth. Pour mixture into a large bowl and cool 10 minutes. Stir in sugar, vanilla and almond extract. Add eggs, one at a time, beating well after each addition until mixture is glossy and smooth. In a small bowl, sift together flour, cocoa, baking powder and salt; add to chocolate mixture, beating just until combined. Spoon batter evenly among pans, filling cups about ⅔ full. Bake 12 minutes or until brownies test done. Cool completely.

In a small bowl, soften gelatin in ¼ cup cold water; let stand for 2 minutes. Add ⅓ cup boiling water, stirring until gelatin dissolves. In a medium mixing bowl, beat cream on high speed until foamy. Gradually add sugar, beating until soft peaks form. Gently stir in gelatin mixture, raspberries and raspberry juice. Cover and chill for 2 hours. Before serving, spoon or pipe raspberry mousse on each brownie, swirling as desired.

Variation

Decorated Brownies

Turn the baked brownies upside down on waxed paper, flattening tops slightly so they rest flat. In a small bowl, melt a few white vanilla candy melts. Dip the narrow end of some brownies into the melted candy, spreading smoothly to create an even surface. Cool until set. Decorate all brownies with piped frosting and mini candies or sprinkles, as desired.

Instant Party Platter

Get three great looks from one recipe by baking brownies as directed and then decorating ⅓ of the brownies with the mousse in the main recipe on page 42, ⅓ of the brownies as directed for Decorated Brownies above and ⅓ of the brownies as directed for Brownie Polka Dots on page 44.

Brownie Polka Dots

Makes 2½ to 3 dozen

• Brownies •

1 (19.5 oz.) pkg. traditional
fudge brownie mix

2 eggs

½ C. vegetable oil

1 tsp. vanilla extract

1 C. mini M&Ms baking bits

Topping

Colored decorating icing

Equipment

nonstick mini muffin pan(s)

Preheat oven to 350°. Lightly coat pans with nonstick cooking spray. In a large bowl, combine brownie mix with ¼ cup water, eggs, oil and vanilla. Beat with a spoon for 2 minutes. Stir in baking bits. Spoon batter into muffin pans, filling each cup about ⅔ full. Bake for 10 to 13 minutes or until brownies test done. Cool in pans.

Turn baked brownies upside down on waxed paper, flattening the tops slightly so they rest flat. Squeeze colored icings directly from the tube, piping in circles, until the narrow end of each brownie is covered in a round "dot." Let icing set up for 10 to 15 minutes; then flatten icing with your fingers or by pressing down lightly on it with waxed paper.

Variations •

To make a holiday "ornament" display, top the brownies with red, green and white icings. Decorate with lines, swirls or small dots of contrasting icing to look like tiny Christmas ornaments. Add nonpareils, candy-coated sunflower seeds, sugar sprinkles or small silver dragées to finish each brownie ornament. Set brownies in holiday-themed liners and arrange them in a small gift box to serve or give away.

If preferred, use the "from scratch" brownie recipe on page on 42 or the blond brownie recipe on page 45 to make these polka dots.

Rainbow Blondie Party Pops

Makes about 1½ dozen

Blondies

½ C. butter, softened

¾ C. brown sugar

1 egg white

½ tsp. vanilla extract

1 C. flour

¼ tsp. baking soda

1 C. M&Ms mini baking bits

½ C. chopped pecans

Coating & Garnishes

2 C. white baking chips

1 T. shortening

Nonpareils or mini baking bits (partially crushed, if desired)

Equipment

8 x 8″ baking pan, parchment paper, wooden popsicle sticks

Preheat oven to 350°. Line pan with parchment paper, allowing 2″ to hang over all sides of pan. In a medium mixing bowl, cream butter and sugar on medium speed until light and fluffy. Beat in egg and vanilla. In a small bowl, combine flour and baking soda; add to creamed mixture just until combined. Dough will be stiff. Stir in baking bits and pecans. Spread dough in prepared pan. Bake for 20 to 30 minutes or until blondies test nearly done. Cool completely.

Gripping parchment paper, remove blondies from pan. Cut into 16 squares. Insert a popsicle stick into one cut edge of each square; chill.

Melt white baking chips and shortening in the microwave until smooth. Holding a blondie on a fork over the bowl, spoon melted coating over the top and sides; tap fork lightly against bowl to smooth coating and let excess drip off. Sprinkle with nonpareils or baking bits while wet. Place on cooling rack or waxed paper until coating has set. If desired, carefully coat the bottom of each blondie pop after top and sides are dry.

Lime Cheesecake Mini Tarts

Makes about 6 dozen

Crust

4 oz. cream cheese, softened

1 egg

1 T. fresh lime juice

½ C. butter, melted

1 (18.25 oz.) box French vanilla cake mix

White baking chips

Filling

1 (24.3 oz.) tub prepared lime cheesecake filling*

½ to 1 tsp. finely grated lime peel, optional

Garnishes

Finely shredded lime peel

Dark or semi-sweet chocolate chips, chopped, optional

Chocolate curls, optional

Equipment nonstick mini muffin pan(s)

Preheat oven to 350°. In a medium mixing bowl, beat cream cheese at medium speed until smooth. Reduce speed and add egg, lime juice and butter; beat until combined, about 1 minute. Stir in cake mix with a spoon until well mixed and dough is thick and pliable. Press about 1½ teaspoons of dough into each muffin cup, pressing it up the sides to the top of each cup. Place several white baking chips in each cup. Bake for 6 to 8 minutes or until light golden brown. Cool crusts for 10 minutes before removing from baking pan. Cool completely before filling.

Just before serving, stir lime peel into cheesecake filling, if desired. Spoon or pipe filling into each crust. Garnish with a sprinkling of lime peel, chopped chocolate or chocolate curls as desired. (If filled tarts are refrigerated overnight, crusts will soften.)

* Fill these tarts with any no-bake cheesecake filling such as the mandarin orange filling or mocha filling on pages 26-27.

Variations

Mini Lime Cheesecake Wedges

(Use one or more 4″ springform pans.)

Prepare crust mixture as directed on page 46, but omit the white chips. Press ⅓ cup of dough into the bottom of a 4″ springform pan. (Use as many pans as desired.) Bake crust for 14 minutes or until lightly browned. Cool completely. Spread 1 cup of lime cheesecake filling over the crust and refrigerate for at least 2 hours or overnight before cutting into wedges to serve. Garnish wedges with a dollop of whipped topping and grated chocolate or a chocolate filigree heart or initials as directed on page 60.

Lime Cheesecake Bites

(Use mini muffin pans with paper or foil liners.)

Fit mini muffin pans with paper liners. Prepare crust mixture as directed on page 46, but omit the white chips. Press 1 teaspoonful of dough into the bottom of each paper liner. Bake for 6 to 7 minutes or until lightly browned; cool completely. Before serving, mound lime cheesecake filling into each liner and garnish as desired.

Black&White Cut-Ups

Makes about 4 dozen

Brownies

1 (19.95 oz.) pkg. brownie
mix, any variety

Water, eggs and oil as
directed on package

Coatings

1 C. white baking chips

2 T. shortening, divided

1 C. semi-sweet
chocolate chips

Equipment 9 x 13″ baking pan, parchment paper, 1½″
to 2″ oval cookie cutter, white lollipop sticks

Preheat oven to 325°. Line pan with parchment paper, allowing 2″ to
hang over all sides of pan. Combine brownie mix, water, eggs and oil as
directed on package. Bake brownies according to directions. Let cool.

Gripping parchment paper, remove brownies from pan. Cut as many
oval shapes from the brownies as possible, brushing off crumbs; move
cut-outs to waxed paper. Carefully insert lollipop sticks into one cut side
of each oval as far as possible. Push down slightly on the cut-outs to help
adhere to the stick.

Melt white baking chips and 1 tablespoon shortening in the microwave until smooth. Holding each oval by its stick above the bowl,
carefully spoon the white mixture over half of the top and sides, allowing
the excess to drip off. Repeat as needed until well-covered. Tap gently
against the bowl to distribute coating evenly. Place on waxed paper until
set. Melt chocolate chips and remaining 1 tablespoon shortening in the
microwave until smooth. In the same manner, spoon melted chocolate
over the uncoated parts of each oval until covered. Place on waxed
paper until set.

Fun Tip

*Throw a football-themed party by decorating these brownie
ovals in your favorite team's colors, using colored candy melts
or tinted almond bark.*

Flower Cut-Ups

Using a small flower-shaped cookie cutter (1½″ to 2″),
cut out as many flower shapes from brownies as possible;
brush off crumbs and turn over so the smooth bottom
sides become the tops. Melt yellow candy wafers (or another
color) in the microwave until smooth. Working above a bowl,
hold a flower on a fork and spoon yellow coating over the top
and sides, allowing excess to drip off. Set on waxed paper to dry.
Using white decorating icing in a tube fitted with a small round tip,
draw a flower outline on top of each cut-up. Place a dab of yellow
decorating icing in the center of each flower. *(Tip: Use a toothpick
to slice off a piece of the frosting as it comes out of the tube and gently
press flat.)*

Stars-and-Stripes Cut-Ups

Using star and small rectangular cookie cutters* (1½″ to 2″), cut
out as many shapes from brownies as possible; brush off crumbs
and turn over so the smooth bottom sides become the tops. Using
tubes of red and white decorator icing fitted with a leaf tip, run
lines of icing across the tops of rectangles. Using blue decorator
icing fitted with a star tip, fill in the top
of each star with piped blue
icing stars as shown.

* If these cookie cutters are not available, draw the shapes on
paper to use as a template and cut out with a small sharp knife.

Tiki Bar Volcanoes

Piña Colada

Makes 1½ dozen

Filling

2 (8 oz.) pkgs. cream
cheese, softened

⅔ C. sugar

2 eggs

1 tsp. rum flavoring

¾ C. finely chopped
dried pineapple

¾ C. toasted coconut*

Base&Toppings

1 C. white baking chips

1 T. shortening

16 to 18 coconut
macaroon cookies**

Additional chopped,
dried pineapple and
toasted coconut

Equipment mini cheesecake pan(s)

Preheat oven to 350°. Coat pan with nonstick cooking spray; set aside.
In a medium mixing bowl, beat cream cheese at medium speed until
smooth. Beat in sugar. Reduce speed and add eggs, beating until
blended. Stir in flavoring, pineapple and coconut until well mixed.
Spoon mixture into cheesecake cups, filling about ¾ full. Bake for
18 minutes or until set. Cool completely. Chill for at least 2 hours.

To assemble, remove cheesecakes from pans. Melt baking chips with
shortening in the microwave until smooth. Fasten the bottom of each
cheesecake to the top of a cookie with a little melted mixture. Drizzle
white mixture over the top of each "volcano" and mound some chopped
pineapple and coconut in the center while wet.

* To toast, place coconut in a single layer on a baking sheet. Bake
at 350° for 5 to 8 minutes or until coconut is golden brown.

** Cookies can be purchased or homemade.

Variations

Grasshopper

Make cheesecake as directed, but substitute ½ teaspoon mint flavoring for rum flavoring and add 2 teaspoons crème de menthe ice cream topping. Stir in green food coloring, if desired. Use chocolate wafers for the base in place of macaroons and drizzle melted white chips and fudge topping over the top. Sprinkle with chopped Andes candies.

Strawberry/Raspberry Daiquiri

Make cheesecake as directed, but in addition to rum flavoring, add 1 teaspoon lemon flavoring and 1 teaspoon strawberry or raspberry flavoring. Stir in red food coloring, if desired. Use oatmeal cookies for the base in place of macaroons and drizzle melted white chips and raspberry preserves over the top. Sprinkle with chopped oatmeal cookies.

Instant Party Platter

Make cheesecakes of each flavor from one batch of filling. Simply prepare the filling for Piña Colada, but omit the rum flavoring. Divide filling between three bowls and add reduced amounts of the required flavorings to each bowl. Bake, chill and garnish each flavor as directed.

Triangle Treats

Makes 4 to 6 dozen

Brownies

1 (19.95 oz.) pkg. brownie mix, any variety

Water, eggs and oil as directed on package

Toppings

1 (16 oz.) container cream cheese frosting

¾ C. salted peanuts, coarsely chopped

1 C. creamy peanut butter

1 (12 oz.) pkg. semi-sweet chocolate chips

3 C. crisp rice cereal

Equipment   9 x 13″ nonstick baking pan

Preheat oven to 350°. Lightly coat pan with nonstick cooking spray. Combine brownie mix, water, eggs and oil as directed on package. Bake brownies according to package directions. Cool completely in pan. Frost brownies with cream cheese frosting; sprinkle with peanuts and refrigerate.

Melt peanut butter and chocolate chips in the microwave; stir until smooth. In a large bowl, combine cereal and peanut butter mixture; stir until evenly coated. Spread evenly over frosted bars. Refrigerate until set. Slice into triangle pieces by cutting rows 1¾″ to 2″ wide along the length and width of the pan, then cutting each square in half, diagonally.

Tip

To make slicing easier, run a sharp knife under warm water and dry it off before slicing these brownie triangles.

Tiny Turtle Cheesecakes

Makes about 3 dozen

Crust

1 C. finely crushed graham cracker or Teddy Graham crumbs

1½ T. margarine, melted

Filling

2 (8 oz.) pkgs. cream cheese, softened

½ C. sugar

⅓ C. unsweetened cocoa powder

1 tsp. vanilla extract

2 eggs

Garnishes

36 pecan halves

¾ C. caramel bits

Equipment

nonstick mini muffin pan(s)

Preheat oven to 350°. With a pastry brush or paper towel, coat muffin cups with melted margarine. Divide crumbs evenly among cups and gently shake pans to coat bottoms and sides with crumbs; set aside. In a medium mixing bowl, beat cream cheese at medium speed until smooth. Add sugar, cocoa and vanilla; beat until blended. Reduce speed and beat in eggs until well mixed. Spoon about 1 tablespoon of filling into each muffin cup, filling about ¾ full. Bake for 12 to 15 minutes or until set. Cool in pan for 15 minutes. Run a small knife around edge of each cup to loosen and lift out cheesecakes. Cool for 30 minutes on a wire rack. Cover and chill for at least 1 hour. Before serving, combine caramel bits with 1½ to 2 teaspoons water in a microwave-safe bowl. Cook in 30 second intervals, stirring until smooth and thick. Spoon caramel mixture on each cheesecake and top with a pecan half.

German Chocolate Brownie Pops

Makes 1 to 1½ dozen

Brownies

½ C. butter, softened

1 (4 oz.) bar German's sweet chocolate, chopped

½ C. sugar

1 tsp. vanilla extract

2 eggs

1 C. flour

½ tsp. baking powder

¼ tsp. salt

Topping

2 T. butter

½ C. brown sugar

2 T. corn syrup

2 T. milk

1 C. toasted coconut*

½ C. finely chopped pecans or walnuts

Equipment

nonstick mini cheesecake pan(s), wooden popsicle sticks

Preheat oven to 350°. Lightly coat pan with nonstick cooking spray. In a small saucepan over low heat, melt ½ cup butter and the chocolate, stirring constantly; cool slightly. Add sugar and vanilla; blend well. Add eggs and beat well. In a small bowl, combine flour, baking powder and salt; add to chocolate mixture, stirring well. Spoon batter into pan, filling each cup about ⅔ full. Bake for 14 to 17 minutes or until brownies test nearly done. Cool 5 minutes and then insert a popsicle stick into each brownie; cool completely. Remove brownies from pan by pushing up from the bottom. If they do not remove easily from pan, run a toothpick or small knife around the edges of each cup to loosen brownie.

* To toast, place coconut in a single layer on a baking sheet. Bake at 350° for 5 to 8 minutes or until coconut is golden brown.

In a small saucepan, melt 2 tablespoons butter; add brown sugar, syrup and milk and blend well. Stir in coconut and pecans. Cook until sugar dissolves and mixture is bubbly, stirring constantly. Remove from heat. While topping is still warm, use a damp knife to spread topping around the lower half of each brownie as shown in photo, lightly pressing topping in place; chill.

Variations

Quick Caramel Brownie Pops

Instead of making the boiled topping, melt caramels or caramel bits (with water as directed on package to make thinner consistency) in the microwave until smooth. Frost the sides of each brownie pop as instructed above and press the toasted coconut and nuts into the warm caramel.

Milk Chocolate Brownie Pops

Omit the German chocolate topping and decorate brownie pops with melted milk chocolate chips and chocolate nonpareils or colored sprinkles.

Cookie Dough Brownie Jewels

Makes about 5 dozen

Brownies

1 (22.5 oz.) pkg. brownie mix with chocolate syrup pouch

Water, eggs and oil as directed on package

1 (17.5 oz.) pouch chocolate chip cookie mix

Butter and egg as directed on package

Frosting

1 (16 oz.) container chocolate frosting or Sour Cream Chocolate Frosting (recipe on page 57)

Equipment

9 x 13" baking pan, parchment paper

Preheat oven to 325°. Line pan with parchment paper, allowing it to hang about 2" over the sides of the pan. In a large bowl, combine brownie mix, water, eggs and oil as directed on package. Spread brownie batter in prepared pan. In another bowl, combine cookie mix with butter and egg as directed on pouch. Drop cookie dough by rounded tablespoon evenly over brownie batter; press down lightly. Bake for 35 to 40 minutes or until it tests nearly done; cool completely. Spread frosting over the top and refrigerate about 30 minutes.

Gripping parchment paper, remove cooled brownies from pan and set on a cutting board. Score diagonal lines about 1¼" apart into the frosting in one direction; turn pan and repeat the process, creating a grid of diamond patterns. *(You may wish to draw this out on a sheet of paper first to use as a template or use a diamond-shaped cookie cutter.)*

Tip

This recipe yields many extra pieces along the edges of the pans after cutting into diamond shapes, but don't let them go to waste…these pieces are great for munching or putting over ice cream!

Variations

Try pouches of other cookie mix flavors, such as peanut butter or sugar cookie dough.

Cut brownies into other shapes such as small squares, triangles or strips using a knife or small cookie cutters (1″ to 2″).

Sour Cream Chocolate Frosting

Frosts one 9 x 13″ pan

2 C. semi-sweet
   chocolate chips
½ C. butter
1 C. sour cream

1 tsp. vanilla extract
4½ to 5 C. powdered
   sugar, sifted

In a medium saucepan over low heat, melt chocolate chips and butter. Remove from heat and cool 5 minutes. Place mixture into large bowl and add sour cream and vanilla; mix well. Add powdered sugar and beat until light, fluffy and of desired spreading consistency. Spread frosting on brownies. When cool, cut brownies as directed on page 56. Refrigerate frosted brownies.

Instant Party Platter

Prepare brownie batter and cookie dough as directed for Cookie Dough Brownie Jewels, but spread only half the batter and half the dough in a lined 8 x 8″ baking pan. Bake, frost and cut into small diamonds as directed. Spread remaining brownie batter in a greased 7″ square casserole dish (or 5 x 7″ loaf pan) and bake until brownies test done. Cut cooled brownies into small squares. Shape remaining cookie dough into tiny cookies and bake. Put the assortment of jewels, brownies and cookies on a single platter.

Blueberry Cheesecake Fudge Miniatures

Makes about 4 dozen

Cheesecake Fudge

⅔ C. evaporated milk

2½ C. sugar

5 oz. marshmallow crème

¼ C. butter

1 (3 oz.) pkg. cream cheese, cubed and softened

1 (12 oz.) pkg. vanilla baking chips

1 (4 oz.) pkg. dried blueberries (¾ C.)

1 tsp. vanilla extract

1 tsp. butter flavoring

Garnishes

Whipped topping

Fresh blueberries

Equipment

9 x 9″ nonstick baking pan, mini cupcake liners

Spray pan with nonstick cooking spray, then line the bottom with parchment paper, trimmed to fit. In a medium saucepan over medium heat, warm evaporated milk. Stir in sugar, and slowly bring mixture to a rolling boil, stirring constantly to prevent scorching. Stir in marshmallow crème and butter. Bring mixture back to a full boil and boil for 4½ minutes, stirring constantly. Add cream cheese to the boiling mixture and boil for 1 minute longer. Remove from heat and add baking chips and blueberries. Stir until all chips are melted and mixture is creamy. Stir in vanilla and butter flavoring until well blended. Pour mixture into prepared pan and cool completely before cutting.

To remove from pan, cut around edges of pan with a sharp knife to loosen fudge. Place a cutting board on top of pan and flip over on the board to pop fudge out of pan. Peel off parchment paper, leaving a smooth surface on top. Cut into 1⅛″ squares with a sharp knife or crinkle-cut slicer, or cut out shapes with a small flower or round cookie cutter (1″ to 1½″) coated with nonstick cooking spray. Serve pieces in mini cupcake liners and garnish with whipped topping and blueberries, if desired.

Little Rocky Roads

Makes about 2½ dozen

Brownies

1 C. butter
2 C. semi-sweet
   chocolate chips
1 C. sugar
1 C. brown sugar

1 tsp. salt
4 eggs
1¼ C. flour
1 C. chopped walnuts

Topping

1 C. chopped walnuts
1 C. semi-sweet
   chocolate chips

1½ C. miniature
   marshmallows

Equipment   nonstick mini cheesecake pan(s)

Preheat oven to 350°. Coat pans with nonstick cooking spray. Melt butter
and 2 cups chocolate chips in the microwave until smooth. Stir in sugar,
brown sugar and salt. Add eggs and flour, stirring just until combined.
Mix in 1 cup walnuts. Immediately spoon mixture into prepared pan,
filling each cup about ½ full. Bake for 15 to 17 minutes or until
brownies test nearly done. Remove from oven; sprinkle 1 teaspoon
chopped walnuts, 1 teaspoon chocolate chips and 6 marshmallows on
each brownie. Return to oven; bake until marshmallows are puffed and
lightly browned, 5 to 6 minutes. Cool 5 to 10 minutes. Remove brownies
from pan by pushing up from the bottom. If necessary, run a toothpick
or small knife around each cup to loosen brownie.

Variation

*Line a 9 x 13" pan with foil and coat with nonstick cooking spray.
Spread batter in pan and bake 30 minutes or until brownies test
nearly done. Remove from oven and sprinkle with walnuts,
chocolate chips and marshmallows. Bake until marshmallows are
puffed and lightly browned, 5 to 6 minutes. Cool 5 to 10 minutes.
Remove brownies from pan and cut into small pieces.*

Garnishing with Flair!

Garnishes can turn plain desserts into impressive party-perfect presentations! Just follow these simple instructions and suggestions.

To make chocolate filigrees

Line a baking sheet with waxed paper. In a microwave-safe bowl, melt ¾ cup chocolate candy wafers or almond bark until smooth. Spoon melted chocolate into a plastic bag or waxed paper cone (or use a piping bag with a small round tip). Cut off one corner for piping. Pipe small shapes, such as hearts, free-form designs or letters, on a waxed paper-lined baking sheet. Chill in the freezer for 30 minutes or let stand undisturbed at room temperature until set. Carefully peel the designs off the waxed paper and set them lightly in whipped topping or frosting to garnish the tops of desserts.

To pipe on toppings, mousse or frostings

Fit a plastic piping bag (pastry or decorating) with a large star tip. Fill bag with sweetened whipped cream, whipped topping, mousse or thick frosting. Squeeze bag to pipe desired topping on desserts in patterns, swirls or mounds. To do this with a plastic food storage bag, fill the bag and cut off a medium to large piece from one corner and then squeeze bag to pipe topping.

To drizzle chocolate

Melt ⅓ cup white or dark chocolate chips with ½ teaspoon vegetable oil in a microwave-safe bowl, stirring until smooth. Spoon mixture into a plastic bag and cut a tiny piece off one corner of the bag to drizzle fine lines of chocolate back and forth over the top of desserts.

To add frosted texture to brownies

Coat brownies generously with the frosting and then drag the tines of a fork through it in a back-and-forth or wavy motion to add lines.

To create layers

Slice cheesecakes or brownie cubes into two layers and spread filling or frosting between them. Freeze before coating in chocolate. Garnish as desired.